This book belongs to:

____

Made in the USA
Columbia, SC
06 December 2022

72852933R00061